PREGNANCY COOKBOOK

MEGA BUNDLE – 2 MANUSCRIPTS IN 1 – 80+ Pregnancy– Friendly recipes including, roast, ice-cream, pie and casseroles for a delicious and tasty diet

TABLE OF CONTENTS

ROAST RECIPES 7

ROASTED SQUASH...7

ROASTED CARROT 8

SOUP RECIPES 9

ZUCCHINI SOUP...9

SIDE DISHES 10

CHICKEN NUGGETS 10

BEEF FAJITAS 11

SUMMER SALMON...12

GRILLED SALMON...13

MONKFISH MUSSEL KEBABS 15

POTATO TORTILLA...17

ASIAN STIR-FRY 18

APRICOT CHICKEN PATTIES 19

GREEN PESTO PASTA..20

SALMON WITH ROSEMAY 21

MUSHROOM BURGERS 22

BLACK BEANS BURGERS 24

CABBAGE FRITATTA..26

BRUSSEL SPROUTS FRITATTA 27

CELERY FRITATTA 28

PROSCIUTTO FRITATTA 29

OREGANO FRITATTA 30

HUMMUS WRAP 31

POTATO WEDGES...32

KALE CHIPS 33

EGG ROLL BOWL..34

GREEK BOWL 35

CRANBERRY SALAD 36

GAZPACHO SALAD...37

RADISH & PARSLEY SALAD 38

ZUCCHINI & BELL PEPPER SALAD 39

QUINOA & AVOCADO SALAD 40

TOFU SALAD 41

PAD THAI SALAD...42

AVOCADO SALAD 43

MUSHROOM SALAD 44

MIXED GREENS SALAD 45

QUINOA SALAD 46

STEW RECIPES 47

FISH STEW 47

BUTTERNUT SQUASH STEW 49

CASSEROLE RECIPES..51

BACON CASSEROLE 51

ENCHILADA CASSEROLE 53

PIZZA RECIPES 55

CASSEROLE PIZZA 55

SECOND BOOK 56

BREAKFAST RECIPES 57

PANCAKES 57

BLUEBERRY PANCAKES..58

ALMOND PANCAKES 59

BANANA PANCAKES 60

STRAWBERRY PANCAKES 61

SIMPLE PANCAKES 62

GINGERBREAD MUFFINS 63

BANANA MUFFINS 65

BLUEBERRY MUFFINS 67

STRAWBERRY MUFFINS 69

CHOCOLATE MUFFINS 71

SIMPLE MUFFINS..73

BERRY FRENCH TOAST 74

POHA WAFFLES 75

BREAKFAST BISCUITS...77

INDIAN PANCAKES 78

COOKED MILLET 79

MUFFIN MIX..80

BANANA BREAD 81

FRITTER 83

HOT CHOCOLATE MIX 85

PANCAKE SYRUP...86

PINEAPPLE BREAKFAST CAKE 87

SCRAMBLED EGGS WITH RICE 88

TART RECIPES...89

APPLE TART 89

CHOCHOLATE TART 91

PIE RECIPES 92

PEACH PECAN PIE..92

BLUEBERRY PIE...93

PUMPKIN PIE...94

SMOOTHIE RECIPES 95

GREEN SMOOTHIE...95

WAKE UP SMOOTHIE 96

RASPBERRY SMOOTHIE 97

CHOCOLATE SMOOTHIE 98

PROTEIN SMOOTHIE 99

SUNSHINE SMOOTHIE 100

MANGO SMOOTHIE 101

PEACH SMOOTHIE..102

PUMPKIN SMOOTHIE 103

ICE-CREAM RECIPES 104

COFFE ICE-CREAM 104

STRAWBERRY ICE-CREAM 105

Introduction

Pregnancy   recipes for personal enjoyment but also for family enjoyment. You will love them for sure for how easy it is to prepare them.

ROASTED SQUASH

Serves:	**3-4**
Prep Time:	**10** Minutes
Cook Time:	**20** Minutes
Total Time:	**30** Minutes

INGREDIENTS

- 2 delicata squashes
- 2 tablespoons olive oil
- 1 tsp curry powder
- 1 tsp salt

DIRECTIONS

1. Preheat the oven to 400 F
2. Cut everything in half lengthwise
3. Toss everything with olive oil and place onto a prepared baking sheet
4. Roast for 18-20 minutes at 400 F or until golden brown
5. When ready remove from the oven and serve

Serves: **3-4**
Prep Time: **10**   Minutes
Cook Time: **20**   Minutes
Total Time: **30**   Minutes

INGREDIENTS

- 1 lb. carrot
- 2 tablespoons olive oil
- 1 tsp curry powder
- 1 tsp salt

DIRECTIONS

1. Preheat the oven to 400 F
2. Cut everything in half lengthwise
3. Toss everything with olive oil and place onto a prepared baking sheet
4. Roast for 18-20 minutes at 400 F or until golden brown
5. When ready remove from the oven and serve

ZUCCHINI SOUP

Serves: **4**

Prep Time: **10**   Minutes

Cook Time: **20**   Minutes

Total Time: **30**   Minutes

INGREDIENTS

- 1 tablespoon olive oil
- 1 lb. zucchini
- ¼ red onion
- ½ cup all-purpose flour
- ¼ tsp salt
- ¼ tsp pepper
- 1 can vegetable broth
- 1 cup heavy cream

DIRECTIONS

1. In a saucepan heat olive oil and sauté zucchini until tender
2. Add remaining ingredients to the saucepan and bring to a boil
3. When all the vegetables are tender transfer to a blender and blend until smooth
4. Pour soup into bowls, garnish with parsley and serve

CHICKEN NUGGETS

Serves: *3*

Prep Time: *10*   Minutes

Cook Time: *25*   Minutes

Total Time: *35*   Minutes

INGREDIENTS

- 2 chicken breasts
- ¼ cup almond flour
- 1 tablespoon seasoning
- 1 tablespoon olive oil
- ½ tsp salt
- ¼ tsp pepper

DIRECTIONS

1. Preheat the oven to 375 F
2. In a bowl add seasoning, salt, almond flour, pepper
3. Add pieces of chicken breast into your bowl and cover with flour
4. Transfer to your baking sheet
5. Bake 18-20 minutes, remove and serve

BEEF FAJITAS

Serves: *3*
Prep Time: *10*   Minutes

Cook Time: *20*   Minutes

Total Time: *30*   Minutes

INGREDIENTS

- 1 lb. beef stir-fry strips
- 1 red onion
- 1 red bell pepper
- ¼ tsp tsp cumin
- ¼ tsp chili powder
- salt
- pepper
- 1 avocado

DIRECTIONS

1. In a skillet add strips and stir-fry, add salt, pepper and cook for 2-3 minute and set aside
2. Add onions, bell peppers, chili powder, cumin and fry for 2-3 minutes
3. Remove to a plate and serve with avocado

SUMMER SALMON

Serves: **4**

Prep Time: **10**   Minutes

Cook Time: **30**   Minutes

Total Time: **40**   Minutes

INGREDIENTS

- 3 salmon fillets
- 2 leeks
- 6 oz. asparagus spears
- 1 cup sugar snap peas
- 3 tablespoons white wine
- 1 cup vegetable broth
- 1 tablespoon chives
- salt

DIRECTIONS

1. In a Dutch oven add salmon, asparagus, wine, peas, chicken bean and pepper
2. Bring to boil and simmer for 12-15 minutes
3. Sprinkle with chives and serve

GRILLED SALMON

Serves: **4**

Prep Time: **10** Minutes

Cook Time: **20** Minutes

Total Time: **30** Minutes

INGREDIENTS

- Juice of 1 lime
- 2 tablespoons basil
- 3 salmon fillets
- 2 tablespoons salmon fillets
- 2 cup low-fat yogurt
- 1 tablespoon mayonnaise
- ½ tsp lime zest
- salt
- mixed salad leaves

DIRECTIONS

1. In a bowl mix pepper, basil, lime juice, salt and pepper
2. Add salmon fillets and let it marinade for 20-30 minutes
3. In another bowl mix lime zest, basil, mayonnaise, yogurt and salt
4. Preheat the oven to 400 F and place the salmon fillets on a ridged grill pan

5. Brush the salmon with marinade and grill for 4-5 minutes per side
6. When ready remove and serve

Serves: **12**

Prep Time: **10**   Minutes

Cook Time: **20**   Minutes

Total Time: **30**   Minutes

INGREDIENTS

- 1 lemon
- juice 1 lime
- 1 tablespoon olive oil
- 1 tsp honey
- 1 garlic clove
- 1 tablespoon oregano
- 1 tablespoon parsley
- 6 oz. monkfish fillet
- 12 fresh mussels
- 1 yellow bell pepper
- 1 zucchini
- 12 cherry tomatoes
- salt

DIRECTIONS

1. **In a bowl add lime juice, honey, lemon zest, garlic, oregano and salt and mix well, marinade for 50-60 minutes**

2. Prepare 10-12 wooden skewers and add on each one skewer 1 cube of monkfish, 1 piece of bell pepper, 1 zucchini, 1 mussel and a cherry tomato

3. Grill each kebab for 10-12 minutes or until done

4. When ready, remove and serve

POTATO TORTILLA

Serves: **6**

Prep Time: **10**   Minutes

Cook Time: **20**   Minutes

Total Time: **30**   Minutes

INGREDIENTS

-   1,5 lb. potatoes
-   1 tablespoon olive oil
-   1 red onion
-   1 zucchini
-   1 slice turkey bacon
-   5 eggs
-   1 tablespoon parsley
-   pepper

DIRECTIONS

1. In a saucepan add potato cubes, water and bring to a boil
2. In a skillet add potatoes, bacon, zucchini and cook until potatoes are tender
3. In a bowl beat the eggs, add water, pepper, parsley, pour the egg mixture over the vegetables and cook for 4-5 minutes
4. Slide the tortilla onto a plate, cool for 2-3 minutes and cut into wedges and serve

Serves:	**2**
Prep Time:	**10** Minutes
Cook Time:	**10** Minutes
Total Time:	**20** Minutes

INGREDIENTS

- ½ lb. dried noodles
- 1 lb. Asian stir-fry vegetables
- ½ cups hoisin sauce
- 1 tsp chili flakes

DIRECTIONS

1. In a frying pan add vegetables, water and stir-fry for 4-5 minutes
2. Add hoisin sauce, noodles, chili flakes and toss to coat, remove and serve

Serves: **4**

Prep Time: **10** Minutes

Cook Time: **10** Minutes

Total Time: **20** Minutes

INGREDIENTS

- 1 lb. chicken mince
- 2 slices bread
- 3 oz. pistachio nuts
- 1/3 lb. dried apricots

DIRECTIONS

1. In a bowl mix combine the mince, apricots, bread, pistachios and season with pepper
2. Roll into o4 patties and cook for 4-5 minutes per side
3. Remove and serve

GREEN PESTO PASTA

Serves: **2**
Prep Time: **5**   Minutes

Cook Time: **15**   Minutes

Total Time: **20**   Minutes

INGREDIENTS

- 4 oz. spaghetti
- 2 cups basil leaves
- 2 garlic cloves
- ¼ cup olive oil
- 2 tablespoons parmesan cheese
- ½ tsp black pepper

DIRECTIONS

1. Bring water to a boil and add pasta
2. In a blend add parmesan cheese, basil leaves, garlic and blend
3. Add olive oil, pepper and blend again
4. Pour pesto onto pasta and serve when ready

Serves: **2**
Prep Time: **10** Minutes

Cook Time: **10** Minutes

Total Time: **20** Minutes

INGREDIENTS

- 3 Atlantic salmon fillets
- 2 tsp olive oil
- 1 clove garlic
- 1 tablespoon rosemary
- black pepper
- 1 tablespoon lemon juice
- 1 tablespoon white wine

DIRECTIONS

1. In a frying pan sauté garlic, rosemary and pepper for 1-2 minutes
2. Add fish and cook for 1-2 minutes per side

Serves: **2**

Prep Time: **10**   Minutes

Cook Time: **10**   Minutes

Total Time: **20**   Minutes

INGREDIENTS

- 2 tablespoons olive oil
- 1 lb. mushrooms
- 1 lb. beef mince
- 1 onion
- 1 tsp Worcestershire sauce
- 1 egg
- 4 hamburger buns
- 1 cup lettuce
- 4 slices tomatoes
- salt

DIRECTIONS

1. In a frying pan add mushrooms and cook for 4-5 minutes, remove and set aside
2. In a bowl mix beef mince, salt, pepper, Worcestershire sauce, mushrooms, onion and mix well
3. Form into 2 patties, and refrigerate for 10-15 minutes

4. In a frying pan cook patty for 2-3 minutes per side and also grill hamburger buns
5. Top buns with lettuce, tomatoes and patties
6. Serve when ready

BLACK BEANS BURGERS

Serves: *4*

Prep Time: *10*   Minutes

Cook Time: *20*   Minutes

Total Time: *30*   Minutes

INGREDIENTS

- 1 lb. black beans
- 1 cup brown rice
- 1 onion
- 1 onion
- ¼ tsp tabasco sauce
- 1 egg
- ½ cup bread crumbs
- 5 tablespoons salsa
- 4 hamburger buns
- ½ cups yoghurt
- 4 leaves romaine lettuce
- 1 avocado

DIRECTIONS

1. Preheat the oven to 325 F
2. In a bowl mix mashed beans, onions, tabasco sauce, rice, egg, breadcrumbs and mix well

3. Divide mixture into patties and bake for 12-15 minutes or until done

4. In another bowl mix yoghurt and salsa, serve with lettuce and avocado

Serves: **2**
Prep Time: **10**   Minutes

Cook Time: **20**   Minutes

Total Time: **30**   Minutes

INGREDIENTS

- ½ lb. cabbage
- 1 tablespoon olive oil
- ½ red onion
- 2 eggs
- ¼ tsp salt
- 2 oz. cheddar cheese
- 1 garlic clove
- ¼ tsp dill

DIRECTIONS

1. In a bowl whisk eggs with salt and cheese
2. In a frying pan heat olive oil and pour egg mixture
3. Add remaining ingredients and mix well
4. Serve when ready

BRUSSEL SPROUTS FRITATTA

Serves: **2**
Prep Time: **10**   Minutes

Cook Time: **20**   Minutes

Total Time: **30**   Minutes

INGREDIENTS

- ½ lb. Brussel sprouts
- 1 tablespoon olive oil
- ½ red onion
- ¼ tsp salt
- 2 eggs
- 2 oz. cheddar cheese
- 1 garlic clove
- ¼ tsp dill

DIRECTIONS

1. In a skillet sauté Brussel sprouts until tender
2. In a bowl whisk eggs with salt and cheese
3. In a frying pan heat olive oil and pour egg mixture
4. Add remaining ingredients and mix well
5. Serve when ready

CELERY FRITATTA

Serves: **2**

Prep Time: **10** Minutes

Cook Time: **20** Minutes

Total Time: **30** Minutes

INGREDIENTS

- 1 cup celery
- 1 tablespoon olive oil
- ½ red onion
- ¼ tsp salt
- 2 eggs
- 2 oz. cheddar cheese
- 1 garlic clove
- ¼ tsp dill

DIRECTIONS

1. In a bowl whisk eggs with salt and cheese
2. In a frying pan heat olive oil and pour egg mixture
3. Add remaining ingredients and mix well
4. When ready serve with sautéed celery

PROSCIUTTO FRITATTA

Serves: *2*

Prep Time: *10* Minutes

Cook Time: *20* Minutes

Total Time: *30* Minutes

INGREDIENTS

- 8-10 slices prosciutto
- 1 tsp rosemary
- 1 tablespoon olive oil
- ½ red onion
- ¼ tsp salt
- 2 eggs
- 2 oz. parmesan cheese
- 1 garlic clove
- ¼ tsp dill

DIRECTIONS

1. In a bowl whisk eggs with salt and parmesan cheese
2. In a frying pan heat olive oil and pour egg mixture
3. Add remaining ingredients and mix well
4. When prosciutto and eggs are cooked remove from heat and serve

Serves: **2**
Prep Time: **10**   Minutes

Cook Time: **20**   Minutes

Total Time: **30**   Minutes

INGREDIENTS

- 1 tsp oregano
- 1 tablespoon olive oil
- ½ red onion
- ¼ tsp salt
- 2 eggs
- 2 oz. cheddar cheese
- 1 garlic clove
- ¼ tsp dill

DIRECTIONS

1. In a bowl whisk eggs with salt and cheese
2. In a frying pan heat olive oil and pour egg mixture
3. Add remaining ingredients and mix well
4. Serve when ready

HUMMUS WRAP

Serves: **2**
Prep Time: **5**   Minutes

Cook Time: **5**   Minutes

Total Time: **10** Minutes

INGREDIENTS

- 1 cup cooked brown rice
- 1 gluten-free tortilla
- 2-3 tablespoons hummus
- ¼ cup black beans
- ¼ cup tomatoes
- ¼ cup cucumber
- ¼ cup avocado
- ¼ cup romaine lettuce

DIRECTIONS

1. Microwave the tortilla for 20-30 seconds
2. Spread hummus on tortilla
3. Add beans, tomatoes, cucumber, and remaining ingredients
4. Roll like a burrito and serve

POTATO WEDGES

Serves: **4-6**

Prep Time: **10**   Minutes

Cook Time: **30**   Minutes

Total Time: **40**   Minutes

INGREDIENTS

- 2 white potatoes
- 1 tsp olive oil
- 1 tsp garlic powder
- 1 tsp onion powder
- salt
- 1 cup avocado dip

DIRECTIONS

1. Slice potatoes into thick slices
2. In a bowl combine garlic powder, onion powder, salt, olive oil and mix well
3. Place the potatoes into the mixture and stir to coat
4. Bake the potatoes at 425 F for 25-30 minutes
5. When ready remove from the oven and serve with avocado dip

KALE CHIPS

Serves: **4**

Prep Time: **10** Minutes

Cook Time: **15** Minutes

Total Time: **25** Minutes

INGREDIENTS

- 2 cups kale
- 1 tablespoon avocado oil
- 1 tsp salt
- 1 tsp turmeric
- 1 tsp chili powder
- 1 tsp curry powder

DIRECTIONS

1. In a bowl combine all ingredients except kale
2. Mix well and add kale to the seasoning mixture
3. Toss to coat and then place the kale in a baking dish
4. Bake at 250 F for 12-15 minutes
5. When ready remove from the oven and serve

EGG ROLL BOWL

Serves: **2**

Prep Time: **10**   Minutes

Cook Time: **20**   Minutes

Total Time: **30**   Minutes

INGREDIENTS

- 1 tablespoon olive oil
- 1 clove garlic
- 1 lb. pork
- ½ red onion
- 1 cup carrot
- 1 cabbage
- ½ cup soy sauce
- ¼ tsp black pepper

DIRECTIONS

1. In a skillet sauté garlic and onion until soft
2. Add pork, cabbage and cook for another 6-7 minutes
3. Add soy sauce, carrot and cook until vegetables are tender
4. When ready transfer mixture to a bowl, add pepper and serve

GREEK BOWL

Serves: *1*
Prep Time: *10* Minutes

Cook Time: *20* Minutes

Total Time: *30* Minutes

INGREDIENTS

-   1 tablespoon olive oil
-   1 chicken breast
-   1 tsp oregano
-   1 tsp black pepper
-   1 cup tomatoes
-   ¼ cucumber
-   ¼ cup red onion
-   ¼ cup black olives
-   1/4 cup feta cheese
-   1 cup dressing

DIRECTIONS

1. In a skillet add chicken and cook until golden
2. Add seasoning and onion
3. When ready place all ingredients in a bowl
4. Drizzle dressing on top, mix well and serve

Serves: *2*
Prep Time: *5*   Minutes

Cook Time: *15*   Minutes

Total Time: *20*   Minutes

INGREDIENTS

- ½ cup celery
- 1 packet Knox Gelatin
- 1 cup cranberry juice
- 1 can berry cranberry sauce
- 1 cup sour cream

DIRECTIONS

1. In a pan add juice, gelatin, cranberry sauce and cook on low heat
2. Add sour cream, celery and continue to cook
3. Pour mixture into a pan
4. Serve when ready

Serves: **4**

Prep Time: **10** Minutes

Cook Time: **30** Minutes

Total Time: **40** Minutes

INGREDIENTS

- ½ lb. cherry tomatoes
- ½ cucumber
- 3 oz. cooked quinoa
- 1 tsp bouillon powder
- 2 spring onions
- 1 red pepper
- ½ avocado
- 1 pack Japanese tofu

DIRECTIONS

1. In a bowl combine all ingredients together
2. Add salad dressing, toss well and serve

Serves: **4**

Prep Time: **10**   Minutes

Cook Time: **30**   Minutes

Total Time: **40**   Minutes

INGREDIENTS

- 1 tsp olive oil
- ¼ lb. tomatoes
- 2 oz. radish
- 1 oz. parsley
- 1 tablespoon coriander
- salt

DIRECTIONS

1. In a bowl combine all ingredients together and mix well
2. Add salad dressing, toss well and serve

ZUCCHINI & BELL PEPPER SALAD

Serves: **1**

Prep Time: **5**   Minutes

Cook Time: **5**   Minutes

Total Time: **10**   Minutes

INGREDIENTS

- ¼ cup zucchini
- ¼ cup red capsicum
- ½ cup yellow capsicum
- 1 cup sprouted moong
- ¼ cup apple
- 1 tablespoon olive oil
- 1 tsp lemon juice

DIRECTIONS

1. In a bowl combine all ingredients together and mix well
2. Add olive oil, toss well and serve

Serves: **1**

Prep Time: **5** Minutes

Cook Time: **5** Minutes

Total Time: **10** Minutes

INGREDIENTS

- ¼ cooked quinoa
- ¼ cup avocado
- ¼ cup zucchini
- ¼ cup capsicum cubes
- ¼ cup mushroom
- ½ cup cherry tomatoes
- 1 cup lettuce
- 1 tablespoon sprouts
- 1 tsp olive oil
- Salad dressing

DIRECTIONS

1. In a bowl combine all ingredients together and mix well
2. Add salad dressing, toss well and serve

TOFU SALAD

Serves: **1**

Prep Time: **5** Minutes

Cook Time: **5** Minutes

Total Time: **10** Minutes

INGREDIENTS

- 1 pack tofu
- 1 cup chopped vegetables (carrots, cucumber)

DRESSING

- 1 tablespoon sesame oil
- 1 tablespoon mustard
- 1 tablespoon brown rice vinegar
- 1 tablespoon soya sauce

DIRECTIONS

1. In a bowl combine all ingredients together and mix well
2. Add salad dressing, toss well and serve

PAD THAI SALAD

Serves: *1*

Prep Time: 5   Minutes

Cook Time: 5   Minutes

Total Time: *10*   Minutes

INGREDIENTS

- ¼ lb. rice noodles
- 1 red pepper
- 1 onion
- 4 stalks coriander
- ¼ package silken tofu
- 1 oz. roasted peanuts
- Salad dressing

DIRECTIONS

1. In a bowl combine all ingredients together and mix well
2. Add salad dressing, toss well and serve

AVOCADO SALAD

Serves: **1**

Prep Time: **5** Minutes

Cook Time: **5** Minutes

Total Time: **10** Minutes

INGREDIENTS

- 2 avocados
- ¼ lb. snap peas
- 1 tablespoon sesame seeds

SALAD DRESSING

- 1 tablespoon soya sauce
- 1 tablespoon umeboshi puree
- 2 tablespoons mikawa mirin

DIRECTIONS

1. In a bowl combine all ingredients together and mix well
2. Add salad dressing, toss well and serve

MUSHROOM SALAD

Serves: **1**

Prep Time: **5** Minutes

Cook Time: **5** Minutes

Total Time: **10** Minutes

INGREDIENTS

- ½ lb. mushrooms
- 1 clove garlic
- ½ lb. salad leaves
- ¼ lb. tofu
- 1 oz. walnuts
- salad dressing

DIRECTIONS

1. In a bowl combine all ingredients together and mix well
2. Add salad dressing, toss well and serve

MIXED GREENS SALAD

Serves: *1*

Prep Time: 5   Minutes

Cook Time: 5   Minutes

Total Time: *10*   Minutes

INGREDIENTS

- 2 cucumbers
- 3 radishes
- ¼ red bell pepper
- 2 spring onions
- 1 tablespoon red wine vinegar
- 1 tablespoon rice vinegar
- 1 tablespoon soya sauce
- 1 tablespoon clearspring mirin
- 2 cups mixed salad greens

DIRECTIONS

1. In a bowl combine all ingredients together and mix well
2. Add salad dressing, toss well and serve

QUINOA SALAD

Serves: *1*
Prep Time: 5   Minutes

Cook Time: 5   Minutes

Total Time: *10*   Minutes

INGREDIENTS

- 1 cup cooked quinoa
- ¼ cup clearspring hijiki
- ¼ red bell pepper
- 1 bun watercress
- 2 radishes
- 2 tablespoons goji berries

DIRECTIONS

1. In a bowl combine all ingredients together and mix well
2. Add salad dressing, toss well and serve

FISH STEW

Serves: **4**

Prep Time: **15**   Minutes

Cook Time: **45**   Minutes

Total Time: **60**   Minutes

INGREDIENTS

- 1 fennel bulb
- 1 red onion
- 2 garlic cloves
- 2 tablespoons olive oil
- 1 cup white wine
- 1 tablespoon fennel seeds
- 4 bay leaves
- 2 cups chicken stock
- 8 oz. halibut
- 12 oz. haddock

DIRECTIONS

1. Chop all ingredients in big chunks
2. In a large pot heat olive oil and add ingredients one by one
3. Cook for 5-6 or until slightly brown

4. Add remaining ingredients and cook until tender, 35-45 minutes
5. Season while stirring on low heat
6. When ready remove from heat and serve

BUTTERNUT SQUASH STEW

Serves: **4**

Prep Time: **15**   Minutes

Cook Time: **45**   Minutes

Total Time: **60**   Minutes

INGREDIENTS

- 2 tablespoons olive oil
- 2 red onions
- 2 cloves garlic
- 1. Tablespoon rosemary
- 1 tablespoon thyme
- 2 lb. beef
- 1 cup white wine
- 1 cup butternut squash
- 2 cups beef broth
- ½ cup tomatoes
-

DIRECTIONS

1. Chop all ingredients in big chunks
2. In a large pot heat olive oil and add ingredients one by one
3. Cook for 5-6 or until slightly brown
4. Add remaining ingredients and cook until tender, 35-45 minutes

5. Season while stirring on low heat
6. When ready remove from heat and serve

CASSEROLE RECIPES

BACON CASSEROLE

Serves: **4**

Prep Time: **10** Minutes

Cook Time: **15** Minutes

Total Time: **25** Minutes

INGREDIENTS

- 4-5 slices bacon
- 3-4 tablespoons butter
- 5-6 tablespoons flour
- 2 cups milk
- 3 cups cheddar cheese
- 2 cups chicken breast
- 1 tsp seasoning mix

DIRECTIONS

1. Sauté the veggies and set aside
2. Preheat the oven to 425 F
3. Transfer the sautéed veggies to a baking dish, add remaining ingredients to the baking dish
4. Mix well, add seasoning and place the dish in the oven
5. Bake for 12-15 minutes or until slightly brown

6. When ready remove from the oven and serve

ENCHILADA CASSEROLE

Serves: **4**

Prep Time: **10**   Minutes

Cook Time: **25**   Minutes

Total Time: **35**   Minutes

INGREDIENTS

- 1 tablespoon olive oil
- 1 red onion
- 1 bell pepper
- 2 cloves garlic
- 1 can black beans
- 1 cup chicken
- 1 can green chilis
- 1 can enchilada sauce
- 1 cup cheddar cheese
- 1 cup sour cream

DIRECTIONS

1. Sauté the veggies and set aside
2. Preheat the oven to 425 F
3. Transfer the sautéed veggies to a baking dish, add remaining ingredients to the baking dish
4. Mix well, add seasoning and place the dish in the oven

5. Bake for 15-25 minutes or until slightly brown
6. When ready remove from the oven and serve

CASSEROLE PIZZA

Serves: *6-8*

Prep Time: *10*   Minutes

Cook Time: *15*   Minutes

Total Time: *25*   Minutes

INGREDIENTS

- 1 pizza crust
- ½ cup tomato sauce
- ¼ black pepper
- 1 cup zucchini slices
- 1 cup mozzarella cheese
- 1 cup olives

DIRECTIONS

1. Spread tomato sauce on the pizza crust
2. Place all the toppings on the pizza crust
3. Bake the pizza at 425 F for 12-15 minutes
4. When ready remove pizza from the oven and serve

SECOND BOOK

BREAKFAST RECIPES

PANCAKES

Serves: **4**

Prep Time: **10**   Minutes

Cook Time: **10**   Minutes

Total Time: **20**   Minutes

INGREDIENTS

- 1 cup millet flour
- ½ cup soy flour
- 1 tablespoon baking powder
- ¼ tsp salt
- 1 egg
- 1 cup water
- 2 tablespoons oil

DIRECTIONS

1. In a bowl mix all dry ingredients
2. Stir together all liquids and add to dry ingredients
3. Bake on griddle for 1-2 minutes per side
4. Remove and serve

BLUEBERRY PANCAKES

Serves: *4*
Prep Time: *10*   Minutes

Cook Time: *20*   Minutes

Total Time: *30*   Minutes

INGREDIENTS

- 1 cup whole wheat flour
- ¼ tsp baking soda
- ¼ tsp baking powder
- 1 cup blueberries
- 2 eggs
- 1 cup milk

DIRECTIONS

1. In a bowl combine all ingredients together and mix well
2. In a skillet heat olive oil
3. Pour ¼ of the batter and cook each pancake for 1-2 minutes per side
4. When ready remove from heat and serve

ALMOND PANCAKES

Serves: **4**

Prep Time: **10** Minutes

Cook Time: **30** Minutes

Total Time: **40** Minutes

INGREDIENTS

- 1 cup whole wheat flour
- ¼ tsp baking soda
- ¼ tsp baking powder
- 1 cup almonds
- 2 eggs
- 1 cup milk

DIRECTIONS

1. In a bowl combine all ingredients together and mix well
2. In a skillet heat olive oil
3. Pour ¼ of the batter and cook each pancake for 1-2 minutes per side
4. When ready remove from heat and serve

BANANA PANCAKES

Serves: **4**

Prep Time: **10** Minutes

Cook Time: **20** Minutes

Total Time: **30** Minutes

INGREDIENTS

- 1 cup whole wheat flour
- ¼ tsp baking soda
- ¼ tsp baking powder
- 1 cup mashed banana
- 2 eggs
- 1 cup milk

DIRECTIONS

1. In a bowl combine all ingredients together and mix well
2. In a skillet heat olive oil
3. Pour ¼ of the batter and cook each pancake for 1-2 minutes per side
4. When ready remove from heat and serve

STRAWBERRY PANCAKES

Serves: *4*
Prep Time: *10*   Minutes

Cook Time: *20*   Minutes

Total Time: *30*   Minutes

INGREDIENTS

- 1 cup whole wheat flour
- ¼ tsp baking soda
- ¼ tsp baking powder
- 1 cup strawberries
- 2 eggs
- 1 cup milk

DIRECTIONS

1. In a bowl combine all ingredients together and mix well
2. In a skillet heat olive oil
3. Pour ¼ of the batter and cook each pancake for 1-2 minutes per side
4. When ready remove from heat and serve

SIMPLE PANCAKES

Serves: **4**

Prep Time: **10** Minutes

Cook Time: **30** Minutes

Total Time: **40** Minutes

INGREDIENTS

- 1 cup whole wheat flour
- ¼ tsp baking soda
- ¼ tsp baking powder
- 2 eggs
- 1 cup milk

DIRECTIONS

1. In a bowl combine all ingredients together and mix well
2. In a skillet heat olive oil
3. Pour ¼ of the batter and cook each pancake for 1-2 minutes per side
4. When ready remove from heat and serve

GINGERBREAD MUFFINS

Serves: *8-12*
Prep Time: *10*   Minutes

Cook Time: *20*   Minutes

Total Time: *30*   Minutes

INGREDIENTS

- 2 eggs
- 1 tablespoon olive oil
- 1 cup milk
- 2 cups whole wheat flour
- 1 tsp baking soda
- ¼ tsp baking soda
- 1 tsp ginger
- 1 tsp cinnamon
- ¼ cup molasses

DIRECTIONS

1. In a bowl combine all dry ingredients
2. In another bowl combine all dry ingredients
3. Combine wet and dry ingredients together
4. Fold in ginger and mix well
5. Pour mixture into 8-12 prepared muffin cups, fill 2/3 of the cups

6. Bake for 18-20 minutes at 375 F

7. When ready remove from the oven and serve

BANANA MUFFINS

Serves: *8-12*
Prep Time: *10*   Minutes

Cook Time: *20*   Minutes

Total Time: *30*   Minutes

INGREDIENTS

- 2 eggs
- 1 tablespoon olive oil
- 1 cup milk
- 2 cups whole wheat flour
- 1 tsp baking soda
- ¼ tsp baking soda
- 1 tsp cinnamon
- 1 cup mashed banana

DIRECTIONS

1. In a bowl combine all dry ingredients
2. In another bowl combine all dry ingredients
3. Combine wet and dry ingredients together
4. Fold in mashed banana and mix well
5. Pour mixture into 8-12 prepared muffin cups, fill 2/3 of the cups
6. Bake for 18-20 minutes at 375 F

7. When ready remove from the oven and serve

BLUEBERRY MUFFINS

Serves: *8-12*
Prep Time: *10*   Minutes

Cook Time: *20*   Minutes

Total Time: *30*   Minutes

INGREDIENTS

-   2 eggs
-   1 tablespoon olive oil
-   1 cup milk
-   2 cups whole wheat flour
-   1 tsp baking soda
-   ¼ tsp baking soda
-   1 tsp cinnamon
-   1 cup blueberries

DIRECTIONS

1. In a bowl combine all dry ingredients
2. In another bowl combine all dry ingredients
3. Combine wet and dry ingredients together
4. Fold in blueberries and mix well
5. Pour mixture into 8-12 prepared muffin cups, fill 2/3 of the cups
6. Bake for 18-20 minutes at 375 F

7. When ready remove from the oven and serve

STRAWBERRY MUFFINS

Serves:	*8-12*
Prep Time:	*10* Minutes
Cook Time:	*20* Minutes
Total Time:	*30* Minutes

INGREDIENTS

- 2 eggs
- 1 tablespoon olive oil
- 1 cup milk
- 2 cups whole wheat flour
- 1 tsp baking soda
- ¼ tsp baking soda
- 1 tsp cinnamon
- 1 cup strawberries

DIRECTIONS

1. In a bowl combine all dry ingredients
2. In another bowl combine all dry ingredients
3. Combine wet and dry ingredients together
4. Fold in strawberries and mix well
5. Pour mixture into 8-12 prepared muffin cups, fill 2/3 of the cups
6. Bake for 18-20 minutes at 375 F

7. When ready remove from the oven and serve

CHOCOLATE MUFFINS

Serves: *8-12*

Prep Time: *10*   Minutes

Cook Time: *20*   Minutes

Total Time: *30*   Minutes

INGREDIENTS

- 2 eggs
- 1 tablespoon olive oil
- 1 cup milk
- 2 cups whole wheat flour
- 1 tsp baking soda
- ¼ tsp baking soda
- 1 tsp cinnamon
- 1 cup chocolate chips

DIRECTIONS

1. In a bowl combine all dry ingredients
2. In another bowl combine all dry ingredients
3. Combine wet and dry ingredients together
4. Fold in chocolate chips and mix well
5. Pour mixture into 8-12 prepared muffin cups, fill 2/3 of the cups
6. Bake for 18-20 minutes at 375 F

7. When ready remove from the oven and serve

SIMPLE MUFFINS

Serves: *8-12*
Prep Time: *10*   Minutes

Cook Time: *20*   Minutes

Total Time: *30*   Minutes

INGREDIENTS

- 2 eggs
- 1 tablespoon olive oil
- 1 cup milk
- 2 cups whole wheat flour
- 1 tsp baking soda
- ¼ tsp baking soda
- 1 tsp cinnamon

DIRECTIONS

1. In a bowl combine all dry ingredients
2. In another bowl combine all dry ingredients
3. Combine wet and dry ingredients together
4. Pour mixture into 8-12 prepared muffin cups, fill 2/3 of the cups
5. Bake for 18-20 minutes at 375 F
6. When ready remove from the oven and serve

Serves: 2

Prep Time: 10   Minutes

Cook Time: 15   Minutes

Total Time: 25   Minutes

INGREDIENTS

- 2 bread slices
- 1tsp lemon juice
- 1 tsp vanilla extract
- 2 eggs
- ¼ cup heavy cream
- 1 tsp cinnamon
- ¼ cup maple syrup
- 1 cup blueberries

DIRECTIONS

1. In a bowl combine all ingredients for the dipping
2. Dip the bread slices in the mixture and let them soak for 2-3 minutes
3. When ready fry the bread for 2-3 minutes per side
4. When ready remove from the skillet and serve with blueberries and maple syrup

POHA WAFFLES

Serves: **4**

Prep Time: **10**   Minutes

Cook Time: **10**   Minutes

Total Time: **20**   Minutes

INGREDIENTS

- ½ cup rice flour
- 1 tsp baking soda
- 1 banana
- ½ tsp salt
- 2 tablespoons oil
- ½ cup milk
- 1 tsp cider vinegar
- 1 egg
- ½ cup quinoa flakes
- 1 tablespoon honey

DIRECTIONS

1. In a bowl mix all dry ingredients
2. Separate egg yolk from egg white and beet egg white
3. Mix egg yolk with milk, honey, wet fruit and add dry ingredients to mixture
4. Add cider vinegar and mix gently

5. Pour mixture into waffle iron
6. When remove and serve

BREAKFAST BISCUITS

Serves: **12**

Prep Time: **10** Minutes

Cook Time: **15** Minutes

Total Time: **25** Minutes

INGREDIENTS

- 2 cups flour
- 1 tsp xantham gum
- ½ tsp salt
- 4 tablespoons margarine
- ¾ cup vance's darifree
- 1 tablespoon baking powder
- 1 tsp sugar

DIRECTIONS

1. Preheat oven to 425 F
2. Toss together all ingredients, gather into a ball
3. Form small biscuits and bake for 12-15 minutes
4. Remove and serve

Serves: *2*

Prep Time: *10*   Minutes

Cook Time: *10*   Minutes

Total Time: *20*   Minutes

INGREDIENTS

- 1 cup chick pea flour
- 1 tablespoon ginger
- 1/3 cup chopped green onions
- 1 cu water

DIRECTIONS

1. In a bowl whisk all ingredients together
2. Pour mixture in a pan and cook 1-2 minutes per side
3. Remove and serve with honey

COOKED MILLET

Serves: *4*

Prep Time: *10*   Minutes

Cook Time: *20*   Minutes

Total Time: *30*   Minutes

INGREDIENTS

- 1 cup millet grains
- 3 cups water

DIRECTIONS

1. In a pot toast 1 cup of millet grains until golden brown
2. Add water and bring to boil, stir constantly
3. Cook on low heat for 20 minutes
4. Remove and serve

MUFFIN MIX

Serves: **10**

Prep Time: **10**   Minutes

Cook Time: **20**   Minutes

Total Time: **30**   Minutes

INGREDIENTS

- ¼ cup sugar
- ¼ tsp salt
- ¼ tsp vanilla
- 2 tablespoons shortening
- 1 tablespoon baking powder
- ½ cup milk
- 2 eggs
- 1 cup GF flour mix

DIRECTIONS

1. In a bowl mix together shortening with sugar
2. Sift together the flour, milk, baking powder, salt and beaten eggs
3. Stir in vanilla and pour muffin mixture into muffin cups
4. Bake at 325 F for 15-20 minutes
5. Remove and serve

BANANA BREAD

Serves: **4**

Prep Time: **10** Minutes

Cook Time: **60** Minutes

Total Time: **70** Minutes

INGREDIENTS

- 1 cup soy flour
- 1 ½ tsp baking powder
- ½ tsp xanthan gum
- ½ tsp salt
- ½ cup mashed banana
- 2/4 tsp baking soda
- ½ cup shortening
- ½ cup potato starch flour
- ½ cup rice flour
- 2/3 up honey
- 2 eggs beaten

DIRECTIONS

1. In a bowl mix all dry ingredients together
2. Mix honey and shortening until light and fluffy and add beaten eggs

3. Add dry ingredients with the mashed banana and mix until smooth

4. Pour mixture into a loaf pan and bake for 60 minutes at 325 F

Serves: **4**

Prep Time: **10** Minutes

Cook Time: **20** Minutes

Total Time: **30** Minutes

INGREDIENTS

- 2 cornstarch
- 2 tablespoons rice flour
- 2 packs rise yeast
- 1 egg
- cornstarch bread
- 5 tablespoons potato starch
- 2 tablespoons almonds
- 2 cups water
- 2 tablespoons oil
- 1 tsp salt
- ¼ cup sugar
- 1 tsp xanthan gum

DIRECTIONS

1. In a bowl combine all dry ingredients
2. Add hot water to mixture and beat with a mixer for 4-5 minutes

3. Add oil and beat again for 2-3 minutes
4. Cook until golden brown, remove and serve

HOT CHOCOLATE MIX

Serves: **4**

Prep Time: **10** Minutes

Cook Time: **30** Minutes

Total Time: **40** Minutes

INGREDIENTS

- 4 cups dari-free
- 1 cup sugar
- ¼ tsp salt
- ¾ cup cocoa powder

DIRECTIONS

1. In a bowl mix all ingredients
2. Place 4 tablespoons mix in a cup
3. Add boiling water and stir to dissolve mix

Serves: *4*
Prep Time: *10*   Minutes

Cook Time: *30*   Minutes

Total Time: *40*   Minutes

INGREDIENTS

- 3 cups corn syrup
- 1 cup maple syrup

DIRECTIONS

1. In a jar mix maple syrup with corn syrup
2. 100% pure ingredients are required for this GFCF recipe

PINEAPPLE BREAKFAST CAKE

Serves: **4**

Prep Time: **10**   Minutes

Cook Time: **40**   Minutes

Total Time: **50**   Minutes

INGREDIENTS

- 3 eggs
- 1 tablespoon cinnamon
- 18-ounce can pineapple
- 1 tsp baking soda
- 1 tsp GF vanilla
- 4 ounces GF bread
- ½ cup sugar

DIRECTIONS

1. In a blender add crushed pineapple and the rest of the ingredients, blend until smooth
2. Pour mixture into a pan and sprinkle with cinnamon
3. Bake at 325 F for 40 minutes

Serves: **4**

Prep Time: **10**   Minutes

Cook Time: **10**   Minutes

Total Time: **20**   Minutes

INGREDIENTS

- ¼ cup onion
- ¼ cup margarine
- 4 eggs
- 1/3 cup rice
- ½ tsp salt
- 1 cup grated cheese

DIRECTIONS

1. In a pot cook margarine and onion until golden brown
2. In a bowl mix milk and eggs, add rice, cheese and salt
3. Pour mixture over onion and cook or 4-5 minutes
4. Remove and serve

TART RECIPES

APPLE TART

Serves: **6-8**

Prep Time: **25**   Minutes

Cook Time: **25**   Minutes

Total Time: **50**   Minutes

INGREDIENTS

- pastry sheets

FILLING

- 1 tsp lemon juice
- 3 oz. brown sugar
- 1 lb. apples
- 150 ml double cream
- 2 eggs

DIRECTIONS

5. Preheat oven to 400 F, unfold pastry sheets and place them on a baking sheet
6. Toss together all ingredients together and mix well
7. Spread mixture in a single layer on the pastry sheets
8. Before baking decorate with your desired fruits
9. Bake at 400 F for 22-25 minutes or until golden brown

10. When ready remove from the oven and serve

CHOCHOLATE TART

Serves: **6-8**

Prep Time: **25** Minutes

Cook Time: **25** Minutes

Total Time: **50** Minutes

INGREDIENTS

- pastry sheets
- 1 tsp vanilla extract
- ½ lb. caramel
- ½ lb. black chocolate
- 4-5 tablespoons butter
- 3 eggs
- ¼ lb. brown sugar

DIRECTIONS

1. Preheat oven to 400 F, unfold pastry sheets and place them on a baking sheet
2. Toss together all ingredients together and mix well
3. Spread mixture in a single layer on the pastry sheets
4. Before baking decorate with your desired fruits
5. Bake at 400 F for 22-25 minutes or until golden brown
6. When ready remove from the oven and serve

PEACH PECAN PIE

Serves: **8-12**

Prep Time: **15**   Minutes

Cook Time: **35**   Minutes

Total Time: **50**   Minutes

INGREDIENTS

- 4-5 cups peaches
- 1 tablespoon preserves
- 1 cup sugar
- 4 small egg yolks
- ¼ cup flour
- 1 tsp vanilla extract

DIRECTIONS

1. Line a pie plate or pie form with pastry and cover the edges of the plate depending on your preference
2. In a bowl combine all pie ingredients together and mix well
3. Pour the mixture over the pastry
4. Bake at 400-425 F for 25-30 minutes or until golden brown
5. When ready remove from the oven and let it rest for 15 minutes

BLUEBERRY PIE

Serves: **8-12**

Prep Time: **15**   Minutes

Cook Time: **35**   Minutes

Total Time: **50**   Minutes

INGREDIENTS

- pastry sheets
- ¼ tsp lavender
- 1 cup brown sugar
- 4-5 cups blueberries
- 1 tablespoon lemon juice
- 1 cup almonds
- 2 tablespoons butter

DIRECTIONS

6. Line a pie plate or pie form with pastry and cover the edges of the plate depending on your preference
7. In a bowl combine all pie ingredients together and mix well
8. Pour the mixture over the pastry
9. Bake at 400-425 F for 25-30 minutes or until golden brown
10. When ready remove from the oven and let it rest for 15 minutes

Serves: *8-12*

Prep Time: *15*   Minutes

Cook Time: *35*   Minutes

Total Time: *50*   Minutes

INGREDIENTS

- pastry sheets
- 1 cup buttermilk
- 1 can pumpkin
- 1 cup sugar
- 1 tsp cinnamon
- 1 tsp vanilla extract
- 2 eggs

DIRECTIONS

1. Line a pie plate or pie form with pastry and cover the edges of the plate depending on your preference
2. In a bowl combine all pie ingredients together and mix well
3. Pour the mixture over the pastry
4. Bake at 400-425 F for 25-30 minutes or until golden brown
5. When ready remove from the oven and let it rest for 15 minutes

GREEN SMOOTHIE

Serves: *1*
Prep Time: 5   Minutes

Cook Time: 5   Minutes

Total Time: *10*   Minutes

INGREDIENTS

- 1 banana
- 1 cup pineapple chunks
- 1 cup mango chunks
- 1 cup kale
- 1 cup ice
- ½ cup almond milk

DIRECTIONS

1. In a blender place all ingredients and blend until smooth
2. Pour smoothie in a glass and serve

Serves: **1**

Prep Time: **5** Minutes

Cook Time: **5** Minutes

Total Time: **10** Minutes

INGREDIENTS

- 1 banana
- 1 cup coffee
- ¼ cup milk
- 1 pinch cinnamon
-

DIRECTIONS

1. In a blender place all ingredients and blend until smooth
2. Pour smoothie in a glass and serve

RASPBERRY SMOOTHIE

Serves: *1*
Prep Time: *5*   Minutes

Cook Time: *5*   Minutes

Total Time: *10*   Minutes

INGREDIENTS

- 1 cup raspberries
- ½ cup coconut milk
- 1 cup mango
- ¼ cup pear juice

DIRECTIONS

1. **In a blender place all ingredients and blend until smooth**
2. **Pour smoothie in a glass and serve**

CHOCOLATE SMOOTHIE

Serves: **1**

Prep Time: **5** Minutes

Cook Time: **5** Minutes

Total Time: **10** Minutes

INGREDIENTS

- 1 banana
- 1 tsp cocoa powder
- 1 cup almond milk
- 1 cup chocolate chips

DIRECTIONS

1. In a blender place all ingredients and blend until smooth
2. Pour smoothie in a glass and serve

PROTEIN SMOOTHIE

Serves: *1*

Prep Time: 5   Minutes

Cook Time: 5   Minutes

Total Time: *10*   Minutes

INGREDIENTS

- ¼ avocado
- ¼ cup Greek Yogurt
- 1 tablespoon honey
- 1 cup low-fat milk
- 1 cup ice
- ¼ cup spinach

DIRECTIONS

1. In a blender place all ingredients and blend until smooth
2. Pour smoothie in a glass and serve

Serves: *1*

Prep Time: 5   Minutes

Cook Time: 5   Minutes

Total Time: *10*   Minutes

INGREDIENTS

- 1 banana
- 1 cup almond milk
- Juice from 1 orange
- 1 tablespoon goji berries
- 1 cup ice

DIRECTIONS

1. In a blender place all ingredients and blend until smooth
2. Pour smoothie in a glass and serve

MANGO SMOOTHIE

Serves: **1**

Prep Time: **5** Minutes

Cook Time: **5** Minutes

Total Time: **10** Minutes

INGREDIENTS

- 1 cup mango
- 1 cup spinach
- ¼ avocado
- 1 cup milk
- 1 tsp vanilla extract

DIRECTIONS

1. In a blender place all ingredients and blend until smooth
2. Pour smoothie in a glass and serve

PEACH SMOOTHIE

.

Serves: *1*

Prep Time: 5   Minutes

Cook Time: 5   Minutes

Total Time: *10*   Minutes

INGREDIENTS

- 1 cup almond milk
- 2 peaches
- 1 banana
- 1 cup ice
- 1 tablespoon honey
- 1 tsp almond extract

DIRECTIONS

1. In a blender place all ingredients and blend until smooth
2. Pour smoothie in a glass and serve

PUMPKIN SMOOTHIE

Serves: *1*

Prep Time: *5*   Minutes

Cook Time: *5*   Minutes

Total Time: *10*   Minutes

INGREDIENTS

- ¼ cup oats
- ½ cup puree
- 4 oz. Greek Yogurt
- 1 apple
- ½ cup almond milk
- 1 cup ice

DIRECTIONS

1. In a blender place all ingredients and blend until smooth
2. Pour smoothie in a glass and serve

COFFE ICE-CREAM

Serves: **6-8**

Prep Time: **15** Minutes

Cook Time: **15** Minutes

Total Time: **30** Minutes

INGREDIENTS

- 4 egg yolks
- 1 cup black coffee
- 2 cups heavy cream
- 1 cup half-and-half
- 1 cup brown sugar
- 1 tsp vanilla extract

DIRECTIONS

1. In a saucepan whisk together all ingredients
2. Mix until bubbly
3. Strain into a bowl and cool
4. Whisk in favorite fruits and mix well
5. Cover and refrigerate for 2-3 hours
6. Pour mixture in the ice-cream maker and follow manufacturer instructions

STRAWBERRY ICE-CREAM

Serves: *6-8*

Prep Time: *15*   Minutes

Cook Time: *15*   Minutes

Total Time: *30*   Minutes

INGREDIENTS

- 1 lb. strawberries
- ½ cup sugar
- 1 tablespoon vanilla extract
- 1 cup heavy cram
- 1-pint vanilla

DIRECTIONS

1. In a saucepan whisk together all ingredients
2. Mix until bubbly
3. Strain into a bowl and cool
4. Whisk in favorite fruits and mix well
5. Cover and refrigerate for 2-3 hours
6. Pour mixture in the ice-cream maker and follow manufacturer instructions
7. Serve when ready

THANK YOU FOR READING THIS BOOK!

CPSIA information can be obtained
at www.ICGtesting.com
Printed in the USA
LVHW031754010421
683230LV00001B/20